RAISE YOUR HAND

RUN FOR OFFICE

Christy Mihaly

Rourke

Before Reading: *Building Background Knowledge and Vocabulary*

Building background knowledge can help children process new information and build upon what they already know. Before reading a book, it is important to tap into what children already know about the topic. This will help them develop their vocabulary and increase their reading comprehension.

Questions and Activities to Build Background Knowledge:

1. Look at the front cover of the book and read the title. What do you think this book will be about?
2. What do you already know about this topic?
3. Take a book walk and skim the pages. Look at the table of contents, photographs, captions, and bold words. Did these text features give you any information or predictions about what you will read in this book?

Vocabulary: *Vocabulary Is Key to Reading Comprehension*

Use the following directions to prompt a conversation about each word.

- Read the vocabulary words.
- What comes to mind when you see each word?
- What do you think each word means?

> ### Vocabulary Words:
> - agenda
> - campaign
> - candidates
> - committee
> - office
> - officers
> - page

During Reading: *Reading for Meaning and Understanding*

To achieve deep comprehension of a book, children are encouraged to use close reading strategies. During reading, it is important to have children stop and make connections. These connections result in deeper analysis and understanding of a book.

Close Reading a Text

During reading, have children stop and talk about the following:

- Any confusing parts
- Any unknown words
- Text to text, text to self, text to world connections
- The main idea in each chapter or heading

Encourage children to use context clues to determine the meaning of any unknown words. These strategies will help children learn to analyze the text more thoroughly as they read.

When you are finished reading this book, turn to the next-to-last page for **After Reading Questions** and an **Activity**.

TABLE OF CONTENTS

WHY RUN FOR OFFICE?

Rafael's city is electing a new mayor soon. Rafael attends a public event where three **candidates** take questions from voters. Audience members ask the candidates how they will fix the city's broken water pipes and improve the police department.

The candidates offer different solutions. But all three say if they are elected, they will work hard to make the city a better place. That's why they're running for **office**.

candidates (KAN-di-dates): people running in an election

office (AW-fis): a position of leadership or power

— WHAT NEEDS TO BE FIXED? —

Does your school need playground updates or healthier choices in the cafeteria? Does your community need street repairs or a new garden space? You can run for office to help solve a problem you care about.

Candidates for office ask voters to elect them to solve problems. Is there something in your school or community that needs to be fixed? Are you hoping somebody else will make it right?

What are you waiting for? You can help make change happen. Consider *running for office*.

Running for office doesn't necessarily mean you want to be president of the United States (though someday you could!). Many school and community organizations need people like you to help lead them.

When you run for office, you step up to be a leader. But you won't have to do all the work yourself. Just as a team captain needs the rest of the team to play, a good leader motivates others to work together.

You might think a leader is always forceful. But good leaders also listen to other people's opinions. They investigate problems and solutions. They think creatively.

Above all, good leaders are active community members. They work for positive change. That's why a leader who sees a problem might say, "I'll run for office!"

WHICH OFFICE IS RIGHT FOR YOU?

What office should you run for? You could start with a student organization.

Maybe you're already a member of a school **committee** or group. It probably has **officers** who run the organization. Think about running for one of those positions.

committee (kuh-MIT-ee): a group of people that meets to discuss issues or take actions for a larger group

officers (AW-fi-surz): people who have responsible positions leading an organization

If you're not a member of a school organization, consider joining one. Look for a group that is involved in issues you care about. For instance, maybe you think the school cafeteria should stop using plastic straws. You could talk to your school's environmental committee. You might even decide to run for office in that group.

Another possibility is that your class (or grade) might elect class officers. In many schools, students vote for class president, vice president, and other roles. Class officers work on class activities, such as raising money for dances or class trips. Classes might also elect class representatives for the school-wide student council.

A student council is a student-run school government. Sometimes called student senate, it organizes school activities. The students on the council help shape school policies and identify and solve school problems. Adults participate by offering advice and support.

Student council officers include president, vice president, secretary, and treasurer. Other student officers may oversee special projects. Council committees focus on specific events or issues.

You'll find more opportunities for leadership outside of school. For example, scout troops have patrol leaders. If you're not already part of a community group, explore different local organizations.

Community organizations do many things, from working for equal rights to helping people who need housing, and more. Some groups support local sports teams. Others fight for clean air and water. Some help animals. Others support public libraries or community gardens. Whatever your interest, you can offer a helping hand. And when you're ready, you can run for an office in the organization.

campaign (kam-PAYN): an organized series of actions by someone seeking to win election

——— HIGHER OFFICE ———

Ethan Sonneborn was 13 when he launched his **campaign** for governor of Vermont. Vermont doesn't have an age requirement. Ethan lost but said his 2018 run succeeded because it got people interested in political issues.

—— REPRESENTING ——

The Boston School Committee runs Boston's public schools. Xyra Mercer was elected as the committee's 2021–2022 student representative. She pledged to "include the students' voices that need to be heard" on school issues.

Many community organizations are run by adults. Don't let that stop you! Adults often welcome help from young people.

Some adult-run groups reserve a spot for a student or youth representative. Your local school board or parent-teacher organization might have a student rep. This representative provides input on behalf of other students.

If you'd like to join a group that doesn't have a student representative, you could suggest they add such a position. And then run for it!

Different organizations have different officers. Choosing which office to run for depends on your interests and skills. Which fits you best?

An organization's secretary takes notes at meetings. They may write letters on the organization's behalf. Secretaries should be accurate and organized.

The treasurer keeps track of dues, funds raised, and expenses. They report on the group's finances. Treasurers should be good at budgeting money.

The vice president runs meetings when the president can't. They also may organize the group's calendar and keep records.

The president sets the **agenda** and leads meetings. They coordinate the group's priorities and activities.

agenda (uh-JEN-duh): a list of topics to do or discuss in a meeting

YOUR ELECTION CAMPAIGN

Are you ready to run? When you run for office, you'll ask for people's votes, so it helps if you are comfortable talking with people. Remember that elected officials represent the needs of the people, so being a good listener is important. Ask people what issues they are concerned about. Think about how you can address their concerns.

Running for office might require making speeches. If you're not comfortable speaking to groups of people, you can hone this skill by joining a debate club, participating in poetry slams, or acting in a play. Practice a speech with friends or family. Or talk to yourself in the mirror! Remember to let your personality shine and be yourself.

When the time comes, you'll announce you're running. Sometimes nobody will run against you. But usually, you'll face other candidates. You'll have to convince voters to vote for you. You'll need a campaign.

Think of a catchy campaign slogan. It should summarize who you are and what you'll do if elected. It should tell people why you deserve their vote.

Then talk with voters. Tell them your plans. Listen to them. Explain why they should elect you.

Wherever you're campaigning, check the rules. For example, your school might limit where you can hang posters. Within the rules, tell others about your campaign. You might post signs in the hallways or around town, or make buttons or t-shirts. Spread the word!

VOTE

After the election, once the last vote is counted, a winner is declared.

To the winner: Congratulations! You stepped up. You should be proud. Now the real work begins—good luck to you!

To everyone else: Congratulations! You've won by participating in the process. Keep working on issues you care about. And don't forget, you can run again later.

Interested in politics? Investigate your state's opportunities. Some states have a program in which students run to be Kid Governor. Many states offer legislative **page** programs, allowing students to work with state legislators.

page (payj): a student who helps government lawmakers, mostly by delivering messages and legislative materials

MEMORY GAME

Look at the pictures. What do you remember reading on the pages where each image appeared?

INDEX

AFTER-READING QUESTIONS

1. How could you help your school or community by running for office?
2. Who are three members of your school's student council? If you don't know, how can you find out?
3. Name three offices that you could run for. Why did you choose them and what would you plan to do if elected to one of these offices?
4. Would you like to run for governor of your state? Why or why not?
5. Does your local school board have a student representative? If so, what would you like your rep to tell the board? If not, do you think you could convince your school board to add a student rep?

ACTIVITY

Identify an office you'd like to run for. Write your campaign slogan—a catchy phrase or sentence that captures the reason why you are running and why voters should choose you. It should reflect your strengths as a candidate and let voters know how you'll serve them if elected.

ABOUT THE AUTHOR

Author Christy Mihaly ran for student council several times. She won some elections and lost others. Recently, she has served as board chair of several community organizations. She has published more than thirty books for young readers. A former lawyer, she particularly enjoys writing about government and civics.

© 2023 Rourke Educational Media

www.rourkebooks.com

PHOTO CREDITS: page 1: ©xalanx/Getty Images page 4-5: ©SDI Productions/Getty Images; page 6: ©SDI Productions/Getty Images, ©SIHASAKPRACHUM/Shutterstock; Page 8–9: ©HRAUN/Getty Images;page 10–11: ©M_a_y_a/Getty Images; page 11: ©FangXiaNuo/Getty Images; page 12–13: ©LeoPatrizi/Getty Images; page 14–15: ©Jupiterimages/Getty Images; page 16–17: ©Amir Ridhwan/Shutterstock; page 18–19: ©Jupiterimages/Getty Images; page 19: ©Charles Krupa/The Associated Press; page 20: ©Xyra Mercer; page 20–21: ©SDI Productions/Getty Images; page 23: ©fizkes/Getty Images, ©CatLane/Getty Images; page 24: ©Jupiterimages/Getty Images; page 26–27: ©Image Source/Getty Images; page 28–29: ©arrowsmith2/Getty Images; page 30: ©SDI Productions/Getty Images, ©M_a_y_a/Getty Images, ©Amir Ridhwan/Shutterstock, ©Jupiterimages/Getty Images, ©CatLane/Getty Images, ©Jupiterimages/Getty Images

Edited by: Laura Malay
Cover and interior design by: Nick Pearson

Library of Congress PCN Data

Run for Office / Christy Mihaly
 (Raise Your Hand)
  ISBN 978-1-73165-271-3 (hard cover)(alk. paper)
  ISBN 978-1-73165-243-0 (soft cover)
  ISBN 978-1-73165-301-7 (e-book)
  ISBN 978-1-73165-331-4 (e-pub)
Library of Congress Control Number: 2021952196

Rourke Educational Media
Printed in the United States of America
01-2412211937